MW01016651

My Legacy

My Legacy

Rowan D. McRae

DESTINY IMAGE EUROPE
Via Maiella, 1
66020 San Giovanni Teatino (Ch) - Italy
ISBN: 88-89127-06-6

First printing: 2004

This book and all other Destiny Image Europe books are available at Christian bookstores and distributors worldwide.

To order products, or for any other correspondence:

DESTINY IMAGE EUROPE

Via Acquacorrente, 6
65123 - Pescara - Italy
Tel. +39 085 4716623 - Fax: +39 085 4716622
E-mail: info@eurodestinyimage.com

Or reach us on the Internet:

www.eurodestinyimage.com

Dedication

This book is dedicated to you, the soon-to-be author of your own legacy, and to the people who read it in years to come. Whether they be family or total strangers, may we all learn and grow from the words documented in your book about your life—your legacy.

Table of Contents

Foreword

A well-known archaeologist recently commented that our history was vanishing and wondered if in the not too distant future whether we would have enough historical evidence left to answer questions about our past.

I believe My Legacy is an answer to this possible dilemma.

My own story would fall well within the need to have such a book as this. I am one of the many blessed people to have been adopted as a child and to be loved by an amazing man who, when he married my mother, took on two sons and gave us his name.

Sadly my mother passed away a few years ago; and only one month before her death she gave us, my older brother and me, just enough information for us to find our birth father. I had to wait until I was in my mid-30's before a huge chapter of my own legacy was even known. Even now there are gaps. I certainly know that I have a desire for my own sons to know what my legacy is.

In many cultures throughout the world, the stories of families have been passed from father to son, mother to daughter; and even now many ethnic cultures continue this practice. A book such as My Legacy is an amazing method for families to keep and cherish their roots, stories, and lessons.

Rowan McRae has acted on a strong spiritual urge and written a book that I believe is a gift to all generations on a global scale. It has the potential to bridge gaps, heal broken hearts, answer questions, and rebuild families. As a devoted Christian, Rowan understands the heart of God when it comes to family and encourages people from all walks of life and beliefs to take the opportunity to bring the gift of My Legacy into their homes and families.

Tom Hatch, Pastor
Senior Leader
The Elim Centre, Blenheim
Marlborough, New Zealand

Introduction

On a practical note, you may write as much or as little as you want; it is entirely up to you as this is your book. Make your legacy personal to you, recording the most important things that have happened in your life.

Your experiences can be listed as single events or grouped into categories; in addition, it is your choice if you want to share the "whys" and expand on the reasons. If you feel photos would help, please include them.

Please don't stress yourself trying to recall the memory that equates to the "best" or "worst" of a situation; whatever comes to mind at the time will be perfect.

Enjoy strolling down memory lane, and take a few moments to evaluate how you have spent your time thus far, which will help you to determine how to use whatever time you have left. This journal lends itself to a time of looking back while looking within.

You have the freedom to make it just so—for as it is written, so it is.

Now the Lord is the Spirit, and where the Spirit of the Lord is, there is freedom (2 Corinthians 3:17, emphasis added).

The Gift

To ————————— , my ——————————

   It is with love and my genuine interest and eagerness to know and relate to you better that I ask you to take the time to complete this journal to the best of your ability. I and those who follow in this life will then have a record of the importance and value of your life, and will be able to learn and benefit from what you have experienced

   With all my love, your ——————————— ,

                            Date given: ——————————

The Gift

To _____ , my _____

This is a gift to you—my legacy, a brief summary of my life. I hope that it gives you a better understanding of who I am and provides you with comfort and knowledge for your own journey in life.

With all my love, your _____ ,

Date given: _____

Declaration by Author

This is what I have experienced and know to date. Nothing is written in this book with the intent of hurting anyone who reads it. Quite the contrary, this book has been completed for the purpose of sharing who I truly am and imparting the wisdom that I have learned throughout the course of my life. Hopefully as you read, you will feel and be touched by all the real emotion and sentiment expressed. May you enjoy and learn more about me.

Signed: _____

Date: _____

Physical Facts and Who I Am in the Flesh

Birth

Date of Birth: _____

Time of Birth: _____

Location of Birth: _____

Those Persons Present at My Birth:

_____

_____

_____

_____

_____

"The truth will set you free" (John 8:32).

What I Know About Myself as a Baby

I know very little about my baby and early childhood years because my mother and father had five other children all under six years of age when I arrived. There was little time for specific memories about me. We all just seemed to get rolled into one big "thing"! Perhaps the best notes to write here are those things that a relative or good friend can remember about you as a baby. What kind of baby were you—placid or a real demanding, feed—me-now type? Did you have a favorite toy, pacifier, or blanket? Did you have any favorite foods, eating habits, or habits of any sort? How old were you and what were you like when you first learned to crawl, walk, and talk? These are just a few ideas to get you started. Include anything of interest about yourself from ages 0 through 3 that will give a glimpse of who you were at the beginning of your life. Your descendants may discover and appreciate family likenesses through your writings. Any story is a good story!

_____

_____

_____

_____

_____

_____

_____

_____

_____

_____

"The truth will set you free" (John 8:32).

"The truth will set you free" (John 8:32).

"The truth will set you free" (John 8:32).

"The truth will set you free" (John 8:32).

Death: My Funeral Arrangements

Death has always been somewhat of an interest to me. Actually, I consider it just another stage of life or the next step after life; therefore, I want to have a say in my own funeral arrangements.

Grieving by loved ones at a time such as this is very healing and totally appropriate, and you will want to lighten the burden for those enduring the pain and sadness of a loss by making important decisions now and answering questions like: Do you want to be cremated or buried? This can be an important issue for some people while others don't have a preference. Do you want a funeral service in a church, at the gravesite, or elsewhere? What music do you want to be played or sung? My personal favorite to free the flow of tears from my loved ones is "Time to Say Goodbye" (a duet by Andrea Bocelli and Celine Dion). How much cost will be involved? Do you want an expensive or simple pine casket? Do you want your body to be viewed? Who do you want to serve as pall bearers? Planning and establishing these details can make it so much easier for those left behind as they can simply follow your pre-planned script.

"The truth will set you free" (John 8:32).

9

"The truth will set you free" (John 8:32).

My Thoughts and Understanding of What Will Happen to My Spirit After I Die

(See "The Gold Page")

This is a very personal subject, and I have no idea of what possible theories you may have. But I know for certain that I am off to be with the God who created me and who loves me totally and unconditionally. Fancy that—an eternity of acceptance—not having to try to be anything because you are perfect just as you are. (By the way, that is already the case from God's point of view).

I met my Savior in 2002, and since that time, there have been numerous occasions when God has spoken directly to me. (One instance was regarding this book.) So have faith, take a leap, look at "The Gold Page." And if you are sincere in your intention of acknowledging and giving your life to Jesus, a whole new experience of life will come to you. Believe me, it is richer than we could ever dream of.

_____

_____

_____

_____

_____

_____

_____

"The truth will set you free" (John 8:32).

"The truth will set you free" (John 8:32).

"The truth will set you free" (John 8:32).

The following section is to be completed by the recipient of this book when my time comes to move on.

Date of Death: _____

Time of Death: _____

Location of Death: _____

Those Persons Present at My Death:

_____

_____

_____

_____

_____

"The truth will set you free" (John 8:32).

Family Tree

This section is self-explanatory. I have a great mix of Maori (New Zealand Polynesian) with English on my father's side and German with Scottish on my mother's side—makes for a feisty family!

My Name is: _____

My Mother's Name is: My Father's Name is:

_____   _____

Matriarchal Grandmother	Matriarchal Grandfather	Patriarchal Grandmother	Patriarchal Grandfather
_____	_____	_____	_____
_____	_____	_____	_____
_____	_____	_____	_____
_____	_____	_____	_____

If further ancestry is known, please continue.

_____	_____	_____	_____
_____	_____	_____	_____
_____	_____	_____	_____
_____	_____	_____	_____

"The truth will set you free" (John 8:32).

My Childhood

My Childhood

Were you like me, having only one childhood family home that still remains as your parents' dwelling today? Or did you move frequently during your childhood years?

Describe your home or homes (or perhaps the one you felt most secure in). Was it large or small? What was your room like? Did you have to share a bedroom, or did you have your own space? Did you have a favorite play place or secret hiding place? What were your favorite activities or games?

This will lead your mind back to best friends and adventures, to neighbors and the type of interactions you had with them. Your experiences are part of who you are.

I Grew Up In:

_____

_____

_____

_____

_____

Address(es) and Descriptions of Place(s) That I Lived During My Childhood:

_____

_____

_____

_____

"The truth will set you free" (John 8:32).

My Neighbors Were:

_____
_____
_____
_____
_____
_____
_____
_____
_____

My Best Childhood Friend(s) Were:

_____
_____
_____
_____
_____
_____
_____
_____
_____
_____

"The truth will set you free" (John 8:32).

The Best Time of My Childhood

This time can be a single moment or an entire day or a particular experience, like starting school, attending Girl Scouts or Boy Scouts, playing a sport, riding a horse, spending time with your grandma or grandpa, or any family tradition or outing.

Write about the one special time that you treasure and hold dear to your heart as a childhood memory—something you wouldn't trade for anything.

Sit quietly for a moment and simply let it come to you.

"The truth will set you free" (John 8:32).

"The truth will set you free" (John 8:32).

The Worst Experience During My Childhood

There is no need to dwell any longer on this subject than necessary. You probably already know what it is. Perhaps for you, it is the memory of a lost pet or a friend moving away. For others it may be more serious. Whatever this experience is, take a deep breath and write it down. Take time to cry, grieve for your loss, express your sadness. I will be praying for your healing and that you may find the release that comes only from forgiveness. Your pain may still be acute, but hand all the hurt over to God. Seek compassion and healing in its place. Anyone who has hurt you has probably been hurt themselves or has no clue their actions have had that much impact on you. So take the higher road—be the light. Forgive and free yourself from the hurt.

Now pause for a moment. It is time to let go of what you wrote about. Take another deep breath, make yourself a nice hot cup of your favorite drink relax, and move on.

"The truth will set you free" (John 8:32).

23

"The truth will set you free" (John 8:32).

The Most Useful Lesson I Learned During My Childhood

This topic was easy for me—I learned to work. All my siblings and I have a great work ethic (an important discipline kids need today). This lesson has proven exceptionally useful to me throughout my life as it has often helped me to advance ahead of my peers.

What was it for you? We all come from unique families who are a result of a blend of different people. Each combination teaches us some major life lessons. What was the lesson you learned?

_____

_____

_____

_____

_____

_____

_____

_____

_____

_____

_____

_____

_____

_____

"The truth will set you free" (John 8:32).

"The truth will set you free" (John 8:32).

Knowing What I Know Now, This Is What I Would Do Differently

With maturity comes wisdom, so write a little bit of your wisdom for your grandchildren to read when they are in the early stages of life.

_____

_____

_____

_____

_____

_____

_____

_____

_____

_____

_____

_____

_____

_____

_____

_____

_____

"The truth will set you free" (John 8:32).

"The truth will set you free" (John 8:32).

"The truth will set you free" (John 8:32).

"The truth will set you free" (John 8:32).

My Advice on How to Raise My Grandchildren

Some of you could write an entire book on this topic alone. Personally, I would like my grandchildren raised to be responsible for their actions, to be independent, and to be contributors to society. This means imposed discipline until they learn self-discipline. I have had two shots at raising kids—fortunate or unfortunate as that may be. The first were my husband's three kids who I met when they were ages 7, 11, and 13. (That was 11 years ago.) And now we have a 4 and 8-year-old. Parenting is difficult because kids tend to take whatever liberty we give them to the maximum!

In a word, my advice on raising my grandchildren would be "boundaries"—clear and consistent. It makes for happy kids and a smooth running household. This may be the only shot you get at offering unsolicited advice... so write until your heart is content!

"The truth will set you free" (John 8:32).

"The truth will set you free" (John 8:32).

"The truth will set you free" (John 8:32).

My Experiences

The Funniest Thing I Ever Experienced

Although I have experienced several funny situations, I will share just one sweet memory.

My future husband, his three kids, and I were visiting the zoo. (Our other two children were yet to be born.) We came upon a parrot and were having fun saying things like "Hello" and "Polly want a cracker?" when all of a sudden, the bird said, "Hello" in response. We nearly died of fright and all ruptured into fits of laughter. We have a photo of my husband's and the kids' reactions—it is priceless! Simplistic as this story may seem, it brings joy to my heart each time I recall the scene. So don't underestimate the worth of a "small" tale.

"The truth will set you free" (John 8:32).

"The truth will set you free" (John 8:32).

The Time I Looked Physically the Best

This subject will definitely need photographic evidence from you, just to prove that you were once slim, wrinkle-free, and grew hair in all the right places!

_____

_____

_____

_____

_____

_____

_____

_____

_____

_____

_____

_____

_____

_____

_____

_____

_____

"The truth will set you free" (John 8:32).

"The truth will set you free" (John 8:32).

The Saddest Experience of My Life

This can be anything—death, injury, disappointment, devastating news... Be specific. Write about why this experience caused you to be so sad.

_____

_____

_____

_____

_____

_____

_____

_____

_____

_____

_____

_____

_____

_____

_____

_____

_____

"The truth will set you free" (John 8:32).

"The truth will set you free" (John 8:32).

The Happiest Time in My Life

This can be a specific one-time event or a longer period consisting of many good times. There have been many happy occasions in my life, for instance, the arrival of my children and sharing these experiences with my husband, and sharing the successes of my stepchildren. I remember crying with joy when I watched my oldest stepdaughter compete as a representative of her country, or when my stepson told me of his decision to become a Christian and be baptized, or watching my other stepdaughter's diligence to complete her degree.

Life is rich—with moments of much more value and worth than material things can provide. Some of my happiest moments have been when I am alone, in the midst of singing to my heavenly Father and sharing time with Him. Other happiest times can be those seemingly insignificant afternoons spent gardening or evenings walking the dog with kids flying past on their scooters.

"The truth will set you free" (John 8:32).

43

"The truth will set you free" (John 8:32).

The Most Adventurous Thing I Ever Did

Depending on who you are, this may prove to be an easy one... or perhaps more difficult. Things that may not have seemed that adventurous at the time, may now, with time and perspective, fit this category perfectly. The thought that with adventure often comes risk might help you choose the situation you write about.

"The truth will set you free" (John 8:32).

"The truth will set you free" (John 8:32).

The Most Outrageous Thing I Ever Did

We all have done some crazy things in our time (especially during our naive and impulsive youth), some things of which I now know I would have done differently or not at all. But regret is a waste of time, so give your readers a good laugh and surprise them with your unconventionalism!

"The truth will set you free" (John 8:32).

47

"The truth will set you free" (John 8:32).

The Most Meaningful Thing I Ever Did

This subject can be approached from a few angles. It may pertain to what you have done for society or others, or you may want to write about what you have personally experienced. In 2002, after completing an Alpha course, I formed a personal relationship with Jesus Christ and therefore God. This single event has changed me and provided answers to things that I already knew but didn't know I knew. Believe me, God is real. His instructions regarding how to live our lives are good sensible values that are relevant for today. (I am referring to the ten commandments.) Simply put, they are as follows: 1. No other gods; 2. No idols; 3. Don't misuse God's name; 4. Rest on the Sabbath. 5. Honor your parents; 6. Don't murder; 7. No adultery; 8. Don't steal; 9. Don't lie; 10. Don't covet what others have.

Imagine just for a moment what life would be like if we all followed these simplistic laws.

"The truth will set you free" (John 8:32).

"The truth will set you free" (John 8:32).

"The truth will set you free" (John 8:32).

"The truth will set you free" (John 8:32).

The Time I Felt Closest to God
(See "The Gold Page")

I first suspected that God was real when I held my newborn children for the first time, looked into their little precious faces, and felt like I was looking straight into the eyes of God Himself.

Some six years later, I became a Christian. I have had many moments when I have felt very close to God during my two years walk with Him. Any encounter with excellence or perfection in people I see as an encounter with God. I have never had any intention of writing a book. The idea for this journal came one night directly from Him, and I furiously wrote down on a single piece of paper what was given to me. If you have not yet heard from God, I encourage you to turn to the Gold Page (if you haven't already done so). Once you have opened the doorway to a relationship with God, treat it just like any other relationship—the more time and energy you put forth in the relationship, the more you will receive from that relationship. This category is as much for you as it is for those who will read it in years to come. I encourage you to be open.

_____

_____

_____

_____

_____

_____

_____

_____

_____

"The truth will set you free" (John 8:32).

"The truth will set you free" (John 8:32).

"The truth will set you free" (John 8:32).

"The truth will set you free" (John 8:32).

The Biggest Secret of My Life

This topic may require courage to share, but remember "the truth will set you free." It is important, however, that you choose what is appropriate. Those who may be affected by what you write here are more than likely your loved ones. Hopefully, they love you unconditionally (and if they don't know what that means, it is high time they learned). So whatever you write shouldn't change their love for you. A secret is generally harmful to someone (otherwise, it would not have been kept a secret). In any case, take a risk. If you recall something with the right intention, believe that all will be for good. Chances are they already have an inkling of what you are about to reveal!

_____

_____

_____

_____

_____

_____

_____

_____

_____

_____

_____

_____

_____

"The truth will set you free" (John 8:32).

"The truth will set you free" (John 8:32).

The Most Courageous Thing I Ever Did

Your answer may come easily if you are a fireman, or your answer may be "filling out that last question truthfully!" You may have displayed courage unknowingly at the time you made a decision, like when I fell in love with a man with three kids! Maybe you risked your own safety (perhaps even your life) to save someone else.

The dictionary defines courage as "the ability to do something that frightens one, and/or strength in the face of pain or grief." Perhaps you gave up a secure known situation for a completely new unknown one that required a great deal of perseverance. Or you may have endured great physical pain and found strength to carry on with your life. Do you ever wonder where that strength and courage came from?

_____

_____

_____

_____

_____

_____

_____

_____

_____

_____

_____

"The truth will set you free" (John 8:32).

"The truth will set you free" (John 8:32).

The Biggest Thing I Had to Overcome

This subject could be related to your previous writing on courage, or it could be something completely unrelated. Perhaps you are in the midst of something right now that is a major obstacle.

Remember, in everything in life, you are not alone.

"The truth will set you free" (John 8:32).

"The truth will set you free" (John 8:32).

The Most Humbling Experience I Ever Had

This category is all to do with the realization that you were not as important as you thought you were. For me childbirth was a humbling experience. We all are very important, while at the same time, we are not. Sometimes I think the development of self-esteem has gone too far. There are many people living today who think everything is all about them.

Thinking that someone else's needs are greater than yours and ultimately acting that way, not as a martyr but in an unconditional loving way, is an act of humility. How can you teach humility to your future generations? Share a story you have personally experienced.

"The truth will set you free" (John 8:32).

"The truth will set you free" (John 8:32).

A Major Life Changing Event

The scope of your answer could be vast. There have been several life changing events in my own life, but if I were to choose one, I would list details about landing a job when I was 22 years old with a joint venture business between a USA company and a New Zealand company, that took me to the USA for training. This was my first time away from home.

What major event has influenced your course of life?

_____

_____

_____

_____

_____

_____

_____

_____

_____

_____

_____

_____

_____

_____

_____

"The truth will set you free" (John 8:32).

"The truth will set you free" (John 8:32).

"The truth will set you free" (John 8:32).

"The truth will set you free" (John 8:32).

My Best Friend in My Entire Life

You know who that special person is, whether it be your spouse, a coworker, a schoolmate, a supportive neighbor, a relative, etc.

Explain why you have chosen this person.

_____

_____

_____

_____

_____

_____

_____

_____

_____

_____

_____

_____

_____

_____

_____

_____

_____

"The truth will set you free" (John 8:32).

"The truth will set you free" (John 8:32).

"The truth will set you free" (John 8:32).

"The truth will set you free" (John 8:32).

The Best Job I Ever Had

The reasons for your choices will make this answer and the next answer interesting and beneficial to the future readers of your book.

_____

_____

_____

_____

_____

_____

_____

_____

_____

_____

_____

_____

_____

_____

_____

_____

_____

_____

_____

_____

"The truth will set you free" (John 8:32).

"The truth will set you free" (John 8:32).

The Worst Job I Ever Had

"The truth will set you free" (John 8:32).

"The truth will set you free" (John 8:32).

The Most Important Lesson I Learned in My Work Life

I consider and treat my work each day as though it is my own business. This helps to keep my attention on what is important and makes for a great employee, which then leads to a good employer/employee relationship, which makes for a happy work environment. We all are part of something bigger, and I believe if we give our best wherever possible, the world will be a better place.

"The truth will set you free" (John 8:32).

77

"The truth will set you free" (John 8:32).

The Most Exciting Love or Romance I Ever Had

What made this person so special? How did you feel when you were in their presence? What was so exciting? In addition, answering "why" this love or romance was so exciting will give a greater understanding of you.

_____

_____

_____

_____

_____

_____

_____

_____

_____

_____

_____

_____

_____

_____

_____

_____

_____

_____

"The truth will set you free" (John 8:32).

"The truth will set you free" (John 8:32).

"The truth will set you free" (John 8:32).

"The truth will set you free" (John 8:32).

The Most Important Lesson I Learned in Life

This is another opportunity to pass on some wisdom to future generations. Life is so complicated yet so simple all at the same time—it all depends on your perspective.

How we treat each other and relate to one another has been a recurring lesson in my life. The old adage of "do unto others as you would have them do unto you" has been a great lesson for me. I wonder where that came from? (See Matthew 7:12.)

"The truth will set you free" (John 8:32).

"The truth will set you free" (John 8:32).

The Most Influential Person (or People) in My Life

The "why" is most important here. Your answers can illustrate how people can unwittingly influence a life. Whose life are you influencing?

_____

_____

_____

_____

_____

_____

_____

_____

_____

_____

_____

_____

_____

_____

_____

_____

_____

_____

"The truth will set you free" (John 8:32).

"The truth will set you free" (John 8:32).

"The truth will set you free" (John 8:32).

"The truth will set you free" (John 8:32).

Things I Would Never Have Done if I Knew Then What I Know Today

These answers will help put life into perspective. There are many things that I did in my youthful ignorance that I would like to go back and change; however, my participation in those particular events and activities and even certain thoughts and attitudes are part of my life's journey and helped shape me into who I am today. (I still would like to have missed out on a few of the more unpleasant experiences.) Thank God for forgiveness of self and forgiveness from others.

"The truth will set you free" (John 8:32).

"The truth will set you free" (John 8:32).

Things I Would Have Done More of Knowing What I Know Today

This category can also be used as a guide for future generations. I would be more patient and show greater understanding and empathy of people. I wouldn't make mountains out of mole hills. I would laugh more and dance more.

My motto would be "Don't worry; be happy." (See Matthew 6:25.)

_____

_____

_____

_____

_____

_____

_____

_____

_____

_____

_____

_____

_____

_____

_____

_____

_____

"The truth will set you free" (John 8:32).

"The truth will set you free" (John 8:32).

"The truth will set you free" (John 8:32).

"The truth will set you free" (John 8:32).

Best Piece of Advice I Can Give

Here is another opportunity for you to influence your children, grandchildren, and anyone who reads your journal.

My personal advice is to first put your all into every experience you have. Life is short, and you may never have the same opportunity again. Also appreciate and be grateful for people and circumstances in your life. You're not guaranteed the length of time you have together. Get to know God. This knowledge will develop a whole new aspect of you—your spiritual, less self-absorbed side. It is a great experience, and ultimately you will become a better human being.

"The truth will set you free" (John 8:32).

"The truth will set you free" (John 8:32).

"The truth will set you free" (John 8:32).

My Future

What I Still Want to Achieve or Experience in My Life

Your answers will depend upon your current situation and status in life. You may desire more leisure time, or you may want to get more involved in community life. It could be travel, a business, or more time for family.

This topic will allow you to take a good look at your life and prioritize. You could be more interested in a state of living rather than an actual achievement. No one knows when "your time is up," so maybe it is best to work out the order of importance of what you still want to achieve in your life. Then once you determine the "what," you can decide "how."

_____

_____

_____

_____

_____

_____

_____

_____

_____

_____

_____

_____

"The truth will set you free" (John 8:32).

"The truth will set you free" (John 8:32).

How I Want to Spend Most of My Time for the Remainder of My Life

This topic is also more for your benefit rather than your readers; however, your response will help them to discover where your priorities lie, and they may be able to glean some learning from your choices.

"The truth will set you free" (John 8:32).

"The truth will set you free" (John 8:32).

What I Value Most in Life

I value my relationships the most in life. You can be specific and list individuals and why, or situations and circumstances and why.

_____

_____

_____

_____

_____

_____

_____

_____

_____

_____

_____

_____

_____

_____

_____

_____

_____

_____

"The truth will set you free" (John 8:32).

"The truth will set you free" (John 8:32).

"The truth will set you free" (John 8:32).

"The truth will set you free" (John 8:32).

What I Appreciate Most in Life

At this moment in my life I appreciate the freedoms my husband's success in business gives me, particularly that which allows me to be a full-time mother and gives me the opportunity to place a high priority on our children's lives. In addition, I have been afforded the time to explore and develop who I am in this world and in God, and a time to heal and recover.

So thank you, wonderful husband, for this freedom that is provided to me. Is it a person for you or a situation or circumstance?

Acknowledgment and gratitude makes people's hearts sing, for they realize they matter and are important to someone in life.

"The truth will set you free" (John 8:32).

"The truth will set you free" (John 8:32).

What I Believe God Wants Me to Do With the Remainder of My Life

This is between you and God. If you are unsure, and have received the gift on the Gold Page, then simply spend time and ask God to show you.

I believe God wants me to know Him more, and live my life as best I can to follow the example of His Son. He also wants me to enjoy my life, and experience more fun, laughter, and love. You may have specific guidance from God, or you may just have a feeling. Whatever it is, write it down. This is the moment to stop and seek God's input into the rest of your time here on earth.

_____

_____

_____

_____

_____

_____

_____

_____

_____

_____

_____

_____

_____

"The truth will set you free" (John 8:32).

"The truth will set you free" (John 8:32).

"The truth will set you free" (John 8:32).

"The truth will set you free" (John 8:32).

My Final Thoughts

Take this final opportunity to record anything that you may not have covered already. For me, I would like to thank you for taking the time to complete this journal—a book about your life. It is truly a unique and original work as you yourself are.

May you find healing, happiness, and hope from this experience. God's blessings on you and your loved ones.

Rowan D. McRae

"The truth will set you free" (John 8:32).

"The truth will set you free" (John 8:32).

"The truth will set you free" (John 8:32).

"The truth will set you free" (John 8:32).

The Gold Page

If you are unsure of your situation after you die, take this opportunity to receive the God-given gift of eternal life. Read through the following prayer, then go back and pray it freely and willingly out loud, for as it says in the Scriptures:

That if you confess with your mouth, "Jesus is Lord," and believe in your heart that God raised Him from the dead, you will be saved. For it is with your heart that you believe and are justified, and it is with your mouth that you confess and are saved (Romans 10:9-10).

It is as simple as praying the following words with a heart of truth and willingness. You have nothing to lose and so much to gain.

Heavenly Father, I come to You in the name of Jesus.

I pray and ask Jesus to come into my heart and be Lord over my life.

I believe that Jesus died on the cross for my sins.

Please forgive me for my sins, and transform me into a new person.

I surrender control of my life to You today.

In Jesus' name. Amen.

The Day I Became a Christian:

Date: _____   Signed: _____

"The truth will set you free" (John 8:32).

119

Conclusion

If you prayed this prayer, welcome to God's family.

Listen for God to speak to you through His Holy Spirit. Pray to God and ask Him to show you what He would like you to know and how to find that knowledge. Read a Bible, for the Bible is God's Word and provides us with another way for God to speak to us. Find some other Spirit-filled Christians to talk to. Become a member of a Spirit-filled church.

Although I may not know you, I am committed to praying for all who have prayed this prayer to God, that you may live the reminder of your life as God created you to live. So rest in peace knowing that your destiny in eternity is safe and secure with God. Thanks to Jesus. Amen.

Rowan D. McRae

"The truth will set you free" (John 8:32).

Books to help you grow strong in Jesus

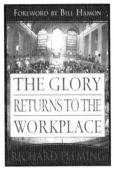

WHERE ARE THE SONS IN THE HOUSE?

By Jerome Nel

Within the church, the concept of mentoring has existed throughout the ages. Spiritual fathers mentor their sons-both men and women-who then become fathers to the next generation. *Where are the Sons in the House?* examines the vital relationship of mentors (spiritual fathers) and mentees (spiritual sons and daughters) in the house of God. This book will allow you to clearly see your role in the local church and will inspire and challenge you to meet your full potential as a member of the body of Christ. This book will open your eyes to the truth of how satan so often manipulates the body of Christ and hinders her growth. If you are serious about becoming who God intends you to be, you must read this book! ISBN:88-89127-01-5

IN MY FATHER'S HOUSE

By Amanda Wells

Too many men of God today are deceived into a building a pedestal, whereby, they have to keep other men from either dethroning them or climbing on board with them. This is not about pride and arrogance. Let it never become about numbers, who has more, but let this apostolic move be about lives and the shaping of men and women into their God-given call and destinies, who leave an inheritance and legacy for our sons and daughters to walk in. ISBN: 88-900588-6-2

TRANSFORMATION AND DOMINION

By Lee LaCoss

Jesus says, "...upon this rock, I will build My church..." In this book we discover many ways that Jesus accomplishes this purpose in and through His people. We are confronted with real questions and issues, and are given practical, biblical answers and direction.

The Lord's "new creation humanity" is called to know Him, and to mature by expressing His nature and abilities as true overcomes in this life.
ISBN: 88-900588-7-0

Order Now from Destiny Image Europe
Telephone: +39 085 4716623- Fax +39 085 4716622
E-mail: ordini@eurodestinyimage.com

Internet: www.eurodestinyimage.com

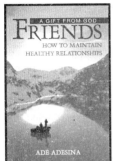

FRIENDS, A GIFT FROM GOD
How to Maintain Healthy Relationships
By Ade Adesina

Relationships are fundamental in the race of life; they can easily be the making or conversely the breaking of any man. All seem to agree that, "no man is an island", however the solution is also often the problem, for the mismanagement of these relationships can negatively impact one's destiny. Many are living frustrated lives because of mismanaged relationships.

Pastor Adesina in this insightful study, expatiates on the nature, purpose and modes of operation of the different types of relationships, and with practical steps, he places in one's hands the tools necessary to enjoy a healthy relaionship with all. It is possible...discover now. ISBN: 88-900588-8-9

SECRETS OF THE MOST HOLY PLACE: VOL. 2
Discovering the Wonders of the Christ within
By Don Nori

Heaven is my destination, but it is not my destiny. Many will reach their destination, but few will achieve their destiny. Prophetic parable matures into prophetic reality as His presence draws us into the realm of 'all God.' Here, what we believe becomes what we experience and what we know becomes flesh in mere mortal man. When we leave Egypt, we leave the bondage we hate, but when we leave the wilderness, we must leave the sin we crave. But He will not condemn what He has redeemed. His Blood covers us until His Power delivers us.

This book is not for the casual reader. It is for those who hunger, not for education, but for reality; not for religion, but for Him. The world awaits the love of a people who know they are forgiven. ISBN: 0768421756

Order Now from Destiny Image Europe
Telephone: +39 085 4716623- Fax +39 085 4716622
E-mail: ordini@eurodestinyimage.com
Internet: www.eurodestinyimage.com

Additional copies of this book and other book titles from DESTINY IMAGE EUROPE are available at your local bookstore.

For a complete list of our titles, visit us at

www.eurodestinyimage.com

Send a request for a catalog to:

Via Maiella, 1
66020 S. Giovanni Teatino (Ch) ITALY